Meditations

from the Iona Community

Ian Reid

First published by Wild Goose Publications, 1998

ISBN 1 901557 02 2

Wild Goose Publications, Unit 15, Six Harmony Row, Glasgow G51 3BA

Wild Goose Publications is the publishing division of the Iona Community.
Scottish Charity No. SC003794.
Limited Company Reg. No SCO96243.

Distributed in Australia and New Zealand by Willow Connection Pty Ltd, Unit 7A, 3-9 Kenneth Road, Manly Vale NSW 2093.

Permission to reproduce any part of this work in Australia or New Zealand should be sought from Willow Connection.

A catalogue record for this book is available from the British Library.

Printed by The Cromwell Press Ltd, Trowbridge, Wilts.
Reprinted 2000, 2004

Contents

In the Presence of God

Worship

Illumination

Death and Resurrection

Support

Serving Others

The Church

Endpiece

Preface

I was invited by the Panel of Worship of the
Church of Scotland to write the prayer guide *Pray
Today* for 1986 - 87. The practice had been to
provide a picture for each day together with a
guide to prayer for that day. I decided that I
would base the guide to prayer on pictures and
that the pictures were those to be found in the
Good News Bible.
Later I offered to produce meditations for
Coracle, the news magazine of the Iona
Community, also based on pictures found in the
Good News Bible.
I have been glad to make them available for
reprinting together by Wild Goose Publications.

Ian Reid

Foreword
The Revd
Ian J. M. Reid
1916 - 1997

As a contribution towards the marking of the Iona Community's sixtieth anniversary in 1998, the Publishing Committee decided to publish a collection of Ian Reid's much-appreciated 'Meditations' which have appeared regularly in *Coracle*. Before this was completed, Ian died in February 1997; so this book is also an expression of the Community's love and thanksgiving for the life of a former Leader.

Ian was the Community's second Leader, from 1967 to 1974, with the unenviable task of taking over from the Founder — with George MacLeod still very much around! Ian carried out his responsibilities with devotion, sensitivity and grace; he combined a strength of commitment to the Gospel and the work of the Iona Community with considerable pastoral gifts and experience and an organizational ability that laid the foundation for the Community's subsequent growth and continuing activities. On the completion of his term of office he returned to a further spell of service in parish ministry at Kilwinning, Ayrshire, distinguished and happily remembered, as were the earlier twenty years in Pilton, Edinburgh. Following his retirement, even when latterly his mobility was much reduced, Ian's ministry of prayer and correspondence continued — supportive and encouraging to so many of his friends. This book is a token of the Community's love for Ian and remembrance of all he contributed to the enrichment of so many lives.

We are grateful to Rosemary Reid for her generous help, and for all she did to support Ian in his ministry and still does on her own; and to Jan Sutch Pickard for completing the editorial work.

It was Ian's intention to begin with a thanksgiving prayer for the life of George MacLeod 'because of my indebtedness to him'. It now seems even more appropriate, in tribute to Ian Reid, to begin with this prayer.

Norman Shanks
Leader of the Iona Community

Be thou, triune God, in the midst of us as we give thanks for those who have gone from the sight of earthly eyes. They, in thy nearer presence, still worship with us in the mystery of the one family in heaven and on earth.

We remember those whom thou didst call to high office, as the world counts high. They bore the agony of great decisions and laboured to fashion the Ark of the Covenant nearer to thy design.

We remember those who, little recognized in the sight of men, bore the heat and burden of the unrecorded day. They served serene because they knew thou hadst made them priests and kings, and now shine as the stars forever.

If it be thy holy will, tell them how we love them, and how we miss them, and how we long for the day when we shall meet with them again.

Prayer by George MacLeod

A Veil Thin As Gossamer

In the Presence of God

The Glories of Creation

Let us recall the times when we have enjoyed the beauties of nature and give thanks to their Creator.

The times when we have enjoyed the mountains and hills; the rounded green hills of the lowlands, and the rugged peaks of the highlands.

The times when we have enjoyed the slow flowing rivers; and the sparkling burns, when we have been refreshed by drinking the cold water or by plunging into the pools.

The times when we have enjoyed the beauty of the green forest trees or the windswept pines.

The times when we have seen birds flying through the sky, the small birds in the garden, the sea birds hopping about the beach, or hovering beside the high cliffs, or diving into the sea or loch.

The times when we have enjoyed nature in company with others.

The times when, on the pilgrimage on Iona, we have both enjoyed the beauties of nature and the community with others, both old friends and new acquaintances.

Everyone has seen what he has done.

Job 36: 25

11

Withdrawal for Prayer

Let us picture Jesus at prayer, both daily and on special occasion:

— in the desert, before his public ministry
— on the hill top, before the choice of his disciples
— in the garden of Gethsemane, before his death.

Let us think of St Columba's Shrine,
and of George MacLeod and the many people
who have prayed there since it was first built.

If we find that the presence of God is unreal for us today, let us recall a place and time when his presence was real. Let us in our imagination return to that time and place that the same experience of the presence of God may become real for us today.

Let us think of all who will enter St Columba's Shrine this coming year and pray that the presence of God may become so real for them that they may be led to pray to him.

Very early the next morning,
long before daylight,
Jesus got up and left the house.
He went out of the town
to a lonely place, where he prayed.

MARK 1: 35

Daniel knew the presence of God by looking to Jerusalem, the place where so often in the past God had become present for him.

If at our time of prayer it is hard to realize the presence of God with us, let us think of where in the past God's presence has been real to us. Let us in our imagination return to such a place, to discover that he is present with us now as we knew his presence then. Such a place might be somewhere in our own home, in our home church, on Iona, on a hill top or beside the sea.

In recognizing the presence of God with us, let us recognize that with him and us are all the saints on earth, including all whom we know.

In looking forward to our death, let us rejoice we will be closer not only to God but also to all those saints with us in heaven, and to those saints still on earth, including those whom we know now.

Personal Prayer

Daniel went home. In an upstairs room of his house there were windows which faced towards Jerusalem. There, just as he had always done, he knelt down at the open windows and prayed to God three times a day.

DANIEL 6: 10

13

The Strength of Fellowship

Let us give thanks for all the times we have received support and strength:

in times of sickness
in times of uncertainty
in times of failure.

Let us give thanks for all the times we have received strength and support: through our association with the Community; through the prayers, words and actions of members and associates, friends and staff of the Community.

Let us give thanks for all the strength and support we have received through members of our families and through friends.

Let us meditate on all the support we can give through our words, and our actions and prayers:

to members of our own families
to members and associates and friends of the Community
to those amongst whom we live and work
to those about whom we hear
through word or writing.

Help others who have all kinds of troubles.

2 Corinthians 1: 4

God's Call

Moses at work as a shepherd, sees a bush alight with flames reaching from earth to heaven. He knows that he is in the presence of God.

'I have indeed heard the cry of my people, and I see how the Egyptians are oppressing them. Now I am sending you to the king of Egypt, so that you can lead my people out of his country.'

Exodus 3: 9, 10

God reveals that he shares in the suffering of his people. He challenges Moses to do something about it.

Moses said, 'I am nobody' ... God answered, 'I will be with you.'

Exodus 3: 11, 12

Moses feels inadequate to do the work he has been challenged to do. God promises to give him strength.

Let us recall the times when unexpectedly we have known the presence of God, and pray that we may be open to experience such times in the future.

Let us think of all people who are suffering today and recall that all such people are God's children and that he is suffering with them.

Let us be open to discover what we can do to bring freedom from suffering.

If the call to relieve such suffering appears to be too difficult, let us remember the promise of God to be with us always.

I am ... This is my name for ever.

Exodus 3: 14 - 15

Quiet Remembering

Mary quietly in meditations remembered all these things.
The promise the angel made to her when her conception was announced:

'Your Son will be great and will be called the Son of the Most High God.'

The promise given by the angels to the shepherds, about her Son:

'This very day in David's town your Saviour was born.'

Mary's life was to be in the background.
She provided the loving home
in which Jesus grew up.
She accepted his leaving home, and the times
when he was too busy to speak to her.
She watched his friends
become smaller in numbers.
She listened to the voices
of the crowds raised in hostility against him.
She saw him die on the cross.

Mary, throughout her life received strength through quietly remembering the promise of the angels.

There is a need for all like Mary, to quietly meditate and to remember all these things.

Mary remembered all these things.

LUKE 2: 19

Worship

Worship

In God's presence we are not alone:
we join with the whole family of God on earth;
we join with men, women and children;
we join with the able, and also with those
handicapped in body or in mind;
we join with those in heaven.

We worship joyfully celebrating:

The existence of God
Beauty in all its forms; the beauty of nature; the
beauty of animals; the beauty of the human form;
the beauty of artistic creation.
God's love for us;
His gift of Jesus;
the readiness of Jesus to love till death;
His glorious resurrection.

We worship humbly in prayer for forgiveness:

Words spoken, action taken without thought or
without love.
Words and actions of support,
unspoken or undone.
Fear of others, or jealousy at their success;
our own failures projected by us on to others.

We worship humbly in prayer for ourselves:

Supplication for our great need — vision and
imagination: to see the world,
and to recognize new possibilities;
to see the work of the Holy Spirit in others;
to know in failure, whether we are right
and must continue or wrong and must change.

We worship humbly in prayer for others:

For the worldwide Church;
for its unity and for its faithfulness
in sharing the Good News;
for its fulfilling of the task of serving the
poor and deprived;for those who can enlarge the
vision of men and women
through their skill in artistic creation.

Come, let us bow down and worship him;
Let us kneel before the Lord our Maker!
He is our God;
we are the people he cares for,
the flock for which he provides.

PSALM 95: 6 - 7

19

Prayer,

Praise the Lord!
Praise the Lord, my soul!
I will praise him as long as I live;
I will sing to God all my life.

Thanksgiving

An old woman lay dying in an Edinburgh tenement. The house was barely furnished. On the floor were strips of old lino, in her bedroom only an old chair and bed. Her husband had died at an early age leaving her with a large family. She bought fish in Musselburgh to carry in a basket, the strap over her head, to sell in Edinburgh. A hard life. She kept on repeating, 'God's been good to me. God's been good to me.'

She had taken nothing for granted.

How much have we taken for granted?
The gift of Jesus; His life of love for men and women; His death on the cross;
His resurrection with its promise of the final victory over evil and death.
His gift of the Holy Spirit,
enabling vision and power.
His inspiration of men and women through the ages, who have passed on the Good News to us.

Count your blessings. Name them one by one.

How much have we taken for granted?
the good things in our own lives;
the love we experienced in childhood in our homes and from others;
the awakening of our minds by the Spirit to truth about God and the world;
the wholeness of body and mind;
The courage to triumph over failure,
disability and suffering.

Count your blessings. Name them one by one.

How much have we taken for granted?
Our inheritance from the past;
the earth whose fertility has been increased through skill and work;
the infrastructure of clean water, safe drainage, and good communications;
buildings for family life, for education,
for entertainment and for work;
knowledge about the universe and the
workings of our bodies;

Jesus said, 'There were ten men who were healed; where are the other nine? Why is this foreigner the only one who came back to give thanks to God?'

LUKE 17: 17 - 18

21

institutions which enable communal living and foster freedom.

Count your blessings. Name them one by one.

Thanksgiving and praise to you, Lord Jesus Christ. Thanks to you for gifts you have given to us. Thank you for our friends and for our life together in the Church. Thank you for life here and for the hope of life to come.

Family Worship

What do we wish for our family?

The opportunity to work? Yes. It is hard to feel part of a society if we cannot make some contribution towards it.

Academic or technical success? Yes. Gifts of mind or hand are wasted if they are not used and developed to the full.

Sporting distinction? Yes. There is satisfaction in skill and success.
Artistic creation? Yes. There is a glory in works of art, giving joy both to the creator and to the receiver.

Money? Yes. There is a need for money to provide for our needs.

Greater than all these is what Paul prayed that his friends at Ephesus might receive: 'I pray that you together with all God's people may have the power to understand how broad and long, how high and deep is God's love. Yes, may you come to know his love — although it can never be fully known — and so be filled with the very nature of God.'

This knowledge of God cannot be taught, it can only be caught — by prayer together at home; prayer together in church.
The family experience together the love of God.
The family together expresses faith in God.

Ever-present Father, we are all your children, members of your family. Help each one of us, when we meet together in the name of Jesus, to know your nearness to us and your love for us. May we come to know you as our Father. Worshipping you may we be drawn closer to one another.

I was glad when they said to me,
'Let us go to the Lord's house.'

PSALM 122: 1

May the God whom my fathers Abraham and
Isaac served bless these boys!
May God, who has led me
to this very day, bless them!

GENESIS 48: 15

Bread of Life

The bird can hover in the sky. The chicks cannot see it, but they are being watched all the time.

At times when God seems to be absent, let us recall that he is watching over us all the time.

The chicks depend on the bird for food.
We depend on spiritual food to give us
vision, wisdom, love and power.
Let us remember that God is offering us
the bread of life.

The chicks have mouths wide open to
receive the food they need to live.
Let us open our lives to receive that bread of life.

Let us pray for all those who are spiritually hungry,
that they may discover God hovering over them
offering them what they need.

Let us pray for the Church, that all its
members may be open
to receive the bread of life,
so that it may be renewed.

... as a bird hovers over its nest.

Isaiah 31: 5

We can use this joyful picture as an inspiration for our praise and thanksgiving to God.

We can recall and give thanks to God for:

The sun	Beautiful sunsets and sunrises; people and events which have given us light after a period of darkness.
The hills	Highland mountains in a wilderness. Lowland hills giving pasture for sheep. Places to which we have retreated to be with God.
The water	The blue water reflects the blue of the sky. Those times when we have seen heaven reflected on earth. The water provides a home for fish. Those who have made us feel at home. The water quenches our thirst. Those who have shared with us the water of life. The water washes away dirt. Those who have given us assurance of acceptance at times of failure and depression.
The flowers	Flowers come to us in a great variety of colour and of form. Those who have captured for us beauty through art. Those who, in all their different personalities, bring us joy.
The birds	Birds freely soaring high into the sky. Those who have risen above prevailing values in society to find new ways to touch the hearts of all, and who have enabled us to join in their flight.

Praise and Thanksgiving

I will praise you, Lord.

PSALM 9: 1

Prayer,

Eternal God,
The sun praises you.
The moon and the stars praise you.

The high hills, the running rivers, the blue lochs,
the wave-tossed ocean praise you.

The tall trees, the wild flowers,
the cultured roses, the green grass,
the life-giving vegetables praise you.

The soaring birds, the wild beasts,
the farm animals, the friendly pets praise you.
The angels, the whole company of heaven,
your whole family on earth, praise you.

We join their praise, we praise you.

Illumination

Growth I

In meditating on growth,

let us ask for forgiveness for failing to recognize
growth coming through those from whom we differ,

let us ask for forgiveness for failing to recognize
that growth comes from God,

let us give thanks for all the growth
we do recognize as coming from God.

In our lives

through our families,
through those whom we have met,
through those whose books we have read,
or whose art has enlightened us.

In the life of the Iona Community

through Iona
through past and present Members,
Associates and Friends.

In the life of the whole Church

through Christians in the past
through Christians today.

In the life of the world

through leaders
through 'unknown' men and women.

I sowed the seed, Apollos watered the plant,
but it was God who made the plant grow.

1 Corinthians 3: 6

The Outsiders

The wise men were foreigners and therefore outsiders. How should outsiders be treated? As servants — or to be served? Jesus tells us that we are no longer servants but sons. The outsiders should be welcomed as brothers.

The wise men came with gifts. They have something to give. A writer has spoken of mission in reverse and has spoken of it as an attitude of reverence for another person, not just a two-way street of equality. It is the reverence for the other person as your teacher.

The wise men came from the East, guided by a star. Is it not surprising that the outsiders saw the star when so many in Israel did not?

Prayer,
Heavenly Father as we go out to others, enable us to know them as brothers and sisters, to listen to them and to learn from them. Give us your Spirit to have the vision of your presence and work in the world.

The same star went ahead of them.

MATTHEW 2: 9 - 10

There is a difference between doing God's will
and rejecting it.
We are not called to accept what people do
which is against God's will.
At times we are called to reject their actions.
This does not mean that we reject them,
as they are still God's children and
therefore our brothers and sisters.

Let us meditate on those groups of people
in the world
whom we consider to be acting against God's will.
Let us affirm each of them as still God's children.
Let us think of any way by which we can warn
them.

Let us meditate on any individuals
whom we consider are rejecting God's will.
Let us affirm each of them as still a child of God.
Let us think of any way by which we can
warn them as a brother or sister.

Let us meditate on any groups
in our district or country
whom we think are rejecting God's way.
Let us affirm them as still God's children.
Let us think of some way
by which we can warn them.

Attitudes Towards Others

Do not treat him as an enemy;
instead, warn him as a brother.

2 THESSALONIANS 3: 15

Thirst
and Dryness

When my people in their need look for water,
when their throats are dry with thirst, then I,
the Lord, will answer their prayer: I, the God
of Israel, will never abandon them. I will make
rivers flow among barren hills and springs of
water run in the valleys. I will turn the desert
into pools of water, and the dry land into
flowing springs.

Isaiah 41: 17, 18

There was no water where they camped, so the
people complained, 'Why have you brought us
into this wilderness? Just so that we can die
here with our animals?' Moses raised the stick
and struck the rock twice with it, and a great
stream of water gushed out, and all the people
and animals drank.

Numbers 20: 2, 4, 11

I travelled along the North African desert. The land was covered with sand and rocks, with the occasional tuft of coarse grass. Day after day the sun shone. From time to time the wind swept the sand into a sandstorm so that it was not possible to see, as in a fog. Suddenly the rain falls. Apparently from nowhere green grass appears, and even wild flowers. The mystery of new life! Cool refreshing rain, after so many days of the heat of the sun! I felt like dancing with joy.

The climber struggles up the steep mountain side on the hot summer day. The further he climbs the hotter he becomes. Sweat pours down his face and over his body. The loss of water makes him more and more thirsty. His tongue and mouth become dry. His whole body cries out for water. The top is reached and the descent begun. It is still as hot as ever. At last he reaches the mountain burn with its cold sparkling water. A drink at last! The thirst is quenched.

The writer looks down at the blank paper. Nothing comes. Will there ever be anything to write? The writer longs for the picture which will be able to convey a message to his readers whoever they may be. He needs to be filled himself if he is going to be able to fill others. At the moment he is like a well with no water in it. Perhaps he has been trying too hard. Perhaps he has been depending too much on his own efforts. Perhaps he needs to be still and quiet and open.

God can make rivers flow. He can turn the desert into pools of water. He can quench the thirst of those who are panting for water.

Prayer,

Father,
You are closer to me
than my own breath.
May each breath I take
deepen the awareness of your presence.

Father,
You are as present and lifegiving as my own heart.
May each heartbeat I experience
deepen my awareness of your presence.

Listening

Have I heard God speaking? I will look back over my life.
In childhood —

> The mystery of worship, watching those sharing in communion.
> The excitement of singing Christmas carols in a decorated church.
> The naturalness of sitting with the family, and looking up the hymns for an aged aunt.
> The challenge to service offered by a youth leader.
> The inspiration of the lives of dedicated men and women who had given their lives to the service of others.
>
> God did speak in childhood.

In the army in North Africa —

> The unexpected sight of a figure in white in the midst of dust, noise and danger: an Anglican chaplain in a white surplice conducting a burial service. A figure in white which spoke of the presence of God in the midst.
> Of one on a cross between two others also on crosses.
>
> The sudden coming of rain — and the desert blossomed.

Holidays which were Holy Days —

> The wildness of the Highlands untouched by man's hand, appearing as God created them.
> The multi-coloured sky as the sun sinks beyond the western horizon.
>
> God did speak through nature.

The Lord came and stood there and called as he had before, 'Samuel! Samuel!' Samuel answered, 'Speak, your servant is listening.'

1 SAMUEL 3: 10

God did speak through the past —

> In places where God has been
> worshipped and his Word has
> been heard through the ages.
> Baptisms in fonts where
> thousands have been baptized
> through the ages.
> Drinking from the same cup which
> Jesus has shared with so many
> through centuries.
> God has spoken through the past.
> But have we always heard?

Prayer,

Ever-present Father, we are quiet; we listen.
The wind speaks to us.
The singing of the birds
speaks to us.
The whistle of the distant
train speaks to us.
The rumble of the
traffic speaks to us.
We hear them now.
You speak to us.
Help us to listen to you.
Help us to hear you.

Watching

The watchman is on the alert for possible attackers.

The devil hides behind what appears to be harmless,
to prevent the watchman from seeing him.
The devil presents what is good in such a way
that the watchman misses the best.
But — the watchman is on the alert
to avoid being deceived by the wiles of the devil.

The watchman is on the alert to see new
opportunities.

His love for the familiar does not blind him to new
and unexpected possibilities.
His attention does not wander
so that he does not miss
new opportunities for service.
He notices the behaviour and expressions
of those whom he meets,
so that he does not miss their cries for help.

The watchman waits for the coming of the morning.

The darkness of the night is menacing.
The bush swaying in the wind
appears like a hostile attacker.
Animals moving through the undergrowth
sound like the footfalls of attacking men.
Will the dawn ever come?

The wait of the watchman is rewarded.
Dawn breaks.
The fears of the night fly away.
The menacing attacker is only a bush.
The sounds of attacking men
were made only by harmless animals.

The Christian watchman is alert to hidden dangers.
He is awake to signs of distress in others.
He notices new opportunities for service.

The Christian watchman is expectantly waiting
for the coming of Jesus,
ready to recognize him in unexpected places
and disguised in unexpected dress.

I wait eagerly for the Lord's help,
and in his word I trust.
I wait for the Lord
more eagerly than watchmen
wait for the dawn.

Psalm 130: 5, 6

esent Father, help us, we pray,
 be awake —
recognize evil,
is present —
cognize when
ing ourselves —
a   needs of others,
to   em their fears and our faith
and
awak   that we do not miss your coming.

Heb. 2

God is Coming

In a time of darkness Good News is wanted — it is urgently needed — it is anxiously awaited.

How strange it is that when it comes it is so often not heard; and if it is heard it is not understood; and if it is understood it is rejected.

The world does not think of the message of the Bible as Good News. God's news is joyful, full of life and hope. So often the world does not perceive the messengers of today as carrying that sort of news.

Good News is positive and life enhancing. So often the news is perceived by the world as negative, as a collection of prohibitions, as life denying.

God is coming! Every day he comes!

The coming of God is feared, because he will bring changes; and changes are feared. It is more comfortable to remain with the familiar.

The coming of God is welcomed. To the outcast, to the oppressed, to the enslaved, the coming of God will bring acceptance, freedom, justice and release.

God comes in weakness, and his coming is despised by the world.

But —
God chooses what the world considers nonsense in order to shame the wise, and he chooses what the world considers to be weak to shame the powerful. He chooses what the world looks down on and despises in order to destroy what the world thinks is important.

Your God is coming. Prepare to welcome him.

Prayer,

Heavenly Father we rejoice that you are continually coming to us. Help us to recognize your coming and to welcome it. Make us ready to follow along new paths. Give us the humility to accept rejection by the world, its laughter and derision, in the knowledge that in the end you will prevail.

Jerusalem, go up on a high mountain
and proclaim the good news!
Call out with a loud voice, Zion;
announce the good news!
Speak out and do not be afraid.
Tell the towns of Judah
that their God is coming!

Isaiah 40: 9

Life in the World

Saul was chosen for his work in the world as king. Can we see our work in the world as service of God? If not — should we be doing it?

Samuel told Saul.
'You will rule his people and protect them from their enemies'. Can we think of our enemies:

Violence
Disease
Starvation
Loneliness

In our work in the world can we protect our people from their enemies?

The anointing of Saul was not only the gift of authority, but also the gift of God's Spirit — the Spirit of wisdom — The Spirit of power.

Do we give enough time to think
of what we are doing?

Do we give space to the coming
of God's inspiration?

Do we remember God's offer of help, which can give us strength to attempt what appears to be outside our reach?

Prayer,

Living God, help us to know the tasks
to which you are calling us in the world
Help us to give time to listen to your voice.
Give us perseverance to continue any task
you have given us until it is completely finished.

Then Samuel took a jar of olive oil and poured it on Saul's head, kissed him and said, 'The Lord anoints you as ruler of his people Israel.'

1 SAMUEL 10: 1

39

Dependence

Jesus got through to that Samaritan woman when she knew that he needed her help.

In a Scottish city a deaconess wanted to make contact with Sikh women. They were very suspicious. She went to the street where many of them lived, and simply stood in it day after day. Time went on and she nearly gave up and went away. One day the rain started to pour and the wind blew hard. A curtain was drawn back, and a Sikh woman looked out. From the same stair a Sikh child came running to invite her inside. She accepted and for the first time entered a Sikh home, to share a cup of tea. The deaconess could only establish communication when she was in the position to receive a gift and not to give one.

It is often harder to receive than to give.

In his humility Jesus was ready to receive.
Lord of all, he depended on men and women.
As a baby, he depended on his mother —
when homeless,
he depended on others for shelter —
when hungry, he depended on gifts of food —
when thirsty, he depended on a woman for a drink.

It is not easy to be dependent.

In disability or old age we may not want
the help we need.
One branch of the Church is not always ready to receive from another — the Church in the West has given and still gives to the Church in Asia and Africa, but it is not always ready to receive from those Churches.

Prayer,

Heavenly Father, give us, we pray, the humility of Jesus. Make us ready and willing to receive from him all that he has to offer. Give us also the grace to receive from others.

A Samaritan woman came to draw some water, and Jesus said to her, 'Give me a drink of water.'

JOHN 4: 7

Joy

One of the greatest marks of the Christian life is joy, because joy is the expression of that life. It is positive and not negative. It is life affirming and not life denying. It is found in the most unexpected places.

It is found in the lives of those who are disabled, who in spite of these very disabilities radiate joy.

It is found in the lives of the poor and of the deprived, who despite their disadvantages have not given up hope.

It is found at funeral services when despite the partial separation of death, there is celebration of a life lived triumphantly to the end. The highlight of one funeral service was the singing of the 'Te Deum': We praise Thee, O God!

It is found in the contemplation of the death of Jesus on the cross.

Prayer,

We thank you Lord, that you did not leave us without your blessing. You have put a new song on our lips and a new joy in our hearts. We praise you for a risen Saviour. We rejoice in a living Lord; and offer our lives in thankful sacrifice to Jesus Christ our Lord.

I am now giving you the choice between life and death, between God's blessing and God's curse, and I call heaven and earth to witness the choice you make. Choose life.

DEUTERONOMY 30: 19

Perseverance

Zacchaeus was desperate to see Jesus. At last he was going to have a chance to do so. He joined the crowds in the street. What a disappointment! He was far too small and was lost in the crowd. He did not give in. However undignified for a man in his position he climbed a tree and received even more than he had ever expected. Jesus came to a meal in his house.

In some parts of the world men and women have witnessed to Jesus with little or no result. It would have been very easy for them to give up, but they laboured on.

In other parts of the world Christians have been disappointed at the response to the work they have been doing. Their disappointment has been increased when they have heard of success elsewhere. It was not easy to remember that no two situations are the same. What appeared to them as failure may in fact have been success.

We are not called to be successful, but faithful.

Prayer,

O Lord God, when thou givest to thy Servants to endeavour any great matter, grant us also to know that it is not the beginning, but the continuing of the same unto the end, until it be thoroughly finished, which yieldeth the true glory, through him who for the finishing of thy work laid down his life, our Redeemer, Jesus Christ.

Prayer of Sir Francis Drake

Zacchaeus was trying to see who Jesus was, but he was a little man and could not see Jesus because of the crowd. So he ran ahead of the crowd and climbed a sycamore tree to see Jesus, who was going to pass that way.

Luke 19: 3, 4

Death and Resurrection

The Garden of Gethsemane

Jesus is the 'Son of God'.
In him we see the true nature of God.

Let us be open to discover what the experience
of Jesus in the garden reveals to us about
the nature of God.

We see him accept the cup of suffering.
He is sharing in all our doubts and sufferings.
He is sharing in the doubts and sufferings of others.

Jesus is the 'Son of Man'.
He reveals to us our true nature.

Let us be open to discover what the experience of
Jesus in the garden had to say about our lives.

Jesus prayed that he might not have to take the cup,
but he took it. This cup he shared with us at
communion.

Jesus prayed and obediently accepted the cup
offered. The disciples slept and at the time of crisis
ran away.

Take this cup of suffering from me!
Yet not what I want but what you want.

MATTHEW 26: 39

Confession

Peter was caught unawares the first time. Later he had even less excuse. Each failure makes it easier to fail the next time.

What about our failures?

Words spoken which are untrue —
sometimes true but unkind.
Words which need not have been spoken.
Word spoken deliberately
which harm and hurt.

Words left unspoken.
Words of apology left unsaid.
Words of apology by others
which have not been accepted.
Words of encouragement
which have not been given.
Sick who have not been visited.
Hungry who have not been fed.
Sinners who have been despised.

Prayer,

Heavenly Father, you know us better
than we know ourselves.
You know our weaknesses and our sins.

You know the words spoken and the actions
undertaken which should never have happened.
You know also how we have failed to speak or act,
when we should have done.

You know how we have taken
pride in our own achievements.
We forget that they have been made
possible only by your Spirit.

Despite all this, you continue to love us.

We acknowledge our sins,
and we accept your forgiveness.

When one of the servant girls saw him sitting there at the fire, she looked straight at him and said, 'This man too was with Jesus!' But Peter denied it, 'Woman, I don't even know him!'

Luke 22: 56, 57

Just then a cock crowed a second time, and Peter remembered how Jesus had said to him, 'Before the cock crows twice, you will say three times that you do not know me.' And he broke down and cried.

Mark 14: 72

46

Three figures: The soldier, Simon, Jesus

The soldier had the right to compel those who were not Roman citizens to carry burdens. He was part of a colonial power. In South Africa we saw white people compelling black people to carry crosses. Was South Africa a microcosm of the whole world, where whites have privileges over blacks?

Like the soldier we confess that we share in the corporate guilt of the privileged world. We have received more that our fair share of the world's goods. We have shared in the imposition
of burdens on others.
Jesus, forgive us.

Simon was forced to carry the cross for Jesus. What were his feelings? Did he later rejoice in the honour that he had been chosen to carry the cross for Jesus?

Like Simon we have been compelled
to carry crosses.
We have carried the burdens of others.
Jesus, forgive our murmuring of complaints.
Jesus, accept our thanks for the privilege of serving others and, in serving them, serving you.

Jesus was handcuffed to the soldier
like a common convict;
he was too physically weak to carry the cross.
Still he identifies himself with convicted prisoners,
and with those who are weak.

Jesus, when we feel condemned,
help us to know you share our guilt.
Where we feel weak
help us to know you share our weakness.

Bearing the Cross I

*They put the cross on him,
and made him carry it.*

LUKE 23: 26

47

Throwing Dice

The soldiers throwing dice for material gain at the foot of the cross are in a different world to Jesus dying at its head.

Let us meditate on how people like the soldiers can be so concerned with material gain, that they are blind to the sufferings of others.

Let us meditate on how we need to be more aware of and sensitive to the needs and sufferings of others.

Jesus at the head of the cross, looks down at those below with loving and forgiving eyes.

Jesus now in heaven is the same Jesus who died on the cross. He still looks down with forgiving eyes.

Let us pray that in our failures we may see the loving and forgiving eyes of Jesus:

— that those who are obsessed with material gain and power may see the loving and forgiving eyes of Jesus

— that our eyes may reflect the loving and forgiving eyes of Jesus.

Then they crucified him ... throwing dice to see who would get which piece of clothing.

MARK 15: 24

What is of Lasting Value?

What in life on earth will disappear with death, and what will be gathered together with all things in Christ?

Let us recognize those things which have no lasting value in our own lives, in the lives of others, and in the life of the world.

Let us rejoice in the eternity

— of our relationship with others

— of creations of beauty, in music, in art, and in writing

— of discoveries of truth

— of actions and words which have enabled God's will to be done on earth even as it is in heaven

This plan, which God will complete when the time is right, is to bring all creation together, everything in heaven and on earth, with Christ as head.

EPHESIANS 1: 10

What did we bring into the world? Nothing! What can we take out of the world? Nothing!

1 TIMOTHY 6: 7

Fear and Loneliness

Men and women can be lonely and afraid:
as members of a small minority in
a state or nation;

when detained or imprisoned unjustly;
in positions of authority,
when motives are suspect;
in the midst of friends,
when faced by conscience to dissent;
in old age,
with no relatives or friends.

What is needed is peace.

On the first Easter evening the disciples were lonely
and afraid. Jesus appeared to them.
He gave them peace.

Jesus still appears to us today.
His word is still the same: 'Peace be with you'.

Heavenly Father, we confess that
all too often we feel lonely and afraid.
Open our eyes to see
the presence of Jesus with us.
Open our ears to hear his word of peace.
Help us to enable others to know his presence,
and to receive his peace.

It was late that Sunday evening, and the disciples were gathered together behind locked doors, because they were afraid of the Jewish authorities. Then Jesus came and stood among them. 'Peace be with you,' he said.

JOHN 20: 19

Look at my hands . . . Stop your doubting, and believe!

JOHN 20: 27

The Ascension

Jesus was parted from them.
He was to be no longer present with
them in the flesh.
He was taken up to heaven,
to be with His Father
who is present everywhere.
He was now to be present with them
in the Spirit at all time and everywhere.
At all times and everywhere Jesus is present
with us, with hands outstretched.

Jesus is present with outstretched hands
shining with light.
In our times of darkness we can take confidence
that he is giving us light.
Others are in darkness,
He is offering them light.

Jesus is present with arms outstretched in love.
In our insecurity he offers us love.
In our hostilities to others
he offers to fill us with love.
To those who feel unloved he offers love.
Those filled with aggression
he offers to fill with love.

Jesus is present with outstretched hands
full of power.
In our weakness he offers strength.
Those who are powerless in any way
— he can enable their action.

As he was blessing them,
he departed from them
and was taken up into heaven.

LUKE 24: 51

Death and Resurrection

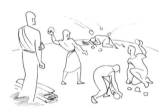

And Saul approved of his murder.

Acts 8: 1

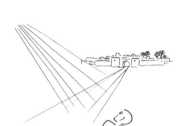

Who are you, Lord?

Acts 9: 5

Saul standing erect and proud — so convinced of his own views and of the danger of new ideas, that he is sure that it is right to kill off Stephen.

Can Saul ever change?

Paul being born to a new life.
No longer arrogant but humbled to the ground.
No longer with a closed mind but open to listen.

Two paths converge on Paul. The light from heaven and the road to the city.
He is blind till he is led to the city to meet Ananias, the Church.
He needed both the personal vision and the fellowship of Ananias, the Church.

What was the content of the vision?
The resurrection.
Jesus is risen in Stephen — in the Church.
The body of the risen Christ is the Church,
The change in Paul is another sign
of the resurrection.

Prayer,

Lord Jesus,
Save us from destroying others by word or action.
Enable us to know that those whom we think your enemies are still your brothers and sisters.
Help us to believe in the possibility of change.
Keep us humble that we may listen.
Knowing the weakness and failings of your church, preserve us from the arrogance of thinking that we do not need it. Keep us open to your word coming to us both directly and through others. Amen.

Paul had been set-up, unjustly judged by the authorities, beaten and imprisoned. The jailer was part of the unjust and persecuting system.

Paul, freed by the earthquake, hearing the despair of the jailer, did not escape but answered the cry of the jailer.

The forgiving love of Paul
changed the life of the jailer.

Let us think of those we see as oppressors of ourselves or of others.

Let us pray for them.

The Power of Forgiving Love

The jailer was about to kill himself. But Paul shouted at the top of his voice, 'Don't harm yourself! We are all here!' The jailer asked, 'Sirs, what must I do to be saved?'

Acts 16: 27 - 30

Support

The Gift of the Dove

Noah keeps watch looking out over the waters, unsure and uncertain. Will the waters ever go down? The dove comes into sight — perhaps the same dove that descended on Jesus at his baptism, the Holy Spirit.

As the dove comes nearer, he sees it carrying from the world a green leaf, the sign of hope — the sign that the long journey in the ark is coming to an end. Noah with open arms receives the gift of the dove — hope.

The dove brings from the world a leaf plucked from an olive branch — the sign of peace and reconciliation.

Noah with open arms receives that promise of peace and reconciliation.

Noah and his family can no longer remain in the ark, the symbol of the Church; they must come out into the world.

The dove still today from the world brings us signs of hope, peace and reconciliation.

Prayer,

Ever-present God, open our eyes to see
the coming of the dove.
As we look over the waters of
our doubts and fears,
enable us to see in the world signs of hope.

As we despair over the injustices and conflicts
in our own lives and in the world,
enable us to see in the world signs of peace and
reconciliation.

As Noah was called to leave the ark and go out into the world, enable us, like him, to share with others the visions of hope, peace and reconciliation we have received.

So Noah knew that the water had gone down.

GENESIS 8: 11

The Healing of Brokenness

Ancient cities depended on walls. Without them Jerusalem was no city.

We can think of ways in which there is brokenness in the universe, in the world community, in our own country, in the Church and in our own lives.

Nehemiah was confident that something could be done, the broken walls could be and were rebuilt. Nehemiah, with the people, gave thanks to God.

We can recall ways in which brokenness has been made whole and we can give thanks.

We can think of ways in which there is still brokenness, and we can express confident hope that the day will come when we can give thanks that wholeness had been given.

I inspected the broken walls.

NEHEMIAH 2: 13

The other group of those who gave thanks went to the left along the top of the wall.

NEHEMIAH 12: 38

The vision of the future: warning and promise.

The vision of fear — a warning:

Destruction of towns and cities
Failure of crops
Diseases in animals
Illness of men and women
Lawlessness and violence
Collapse of economic order.

The content of the picture of fear is the result of the failure of men and women to respond to the love of God and to be open to receive His Spirit.

Does this picture correspond with our fears about the future?

The vision of hope — a promise:

The promised land
A land full of milk and honey.

In faith it is possible to believe that the picture of hope is the picture of the end.

Men and women can change.

The cross was not the end — the resurrection followed. Does this picture correspond with our hope for the future?

Both visions are needed:

The challenge of the warning
The support of the promise.

Two Visions of the Future

But if you disobey the Lord.

DEUTERONOMY 28: 15

The Lord showed him the whole land.

DEUTERONOMY 34: 1

The Empowering God

God is all the time watching over
and guiding his people.
This was true when his people were
slaves in Egypt.
Their situation seemed to be hopeless.
This was true when he guided them
to a new land.

This was true when his people were in exile in
Babylon. Return to their own home appeared to be
hopeless. He watched over them as they
returned home.

Let us meditate on individuals or groups.
For some a new day has dawned.
Let us give thanks.

For others that new day has not yet dawned.
Let us pray that they may be open to God
who is watching over them and
seeking to empower them.
Let us therefore be filled with hope for them.

Let us meditate on the past, present and future:

of our own lives,
of the life of our families,
of the life of the Church,
of the life of our country,
of the life of the world.

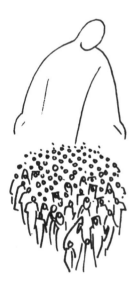

I will bring your people home.

Isaiah 43: 5

Diversity of Gifts

Let us meditate on animals,
the creation of God.

All have gifts which in their diversity
are not always recognized.

The Ostrich,
    she cannot fly,
    but her wings beat fast.
    She was made foolish without wisdom.
    But when she runs
    She can laugh at any horse or rider.

Horses,
    without fear they can rush into battle
    with all their strength.
    With courage they are ready to face danger.

Eagles,
    flying high they can watch near and far.
    They have wide vision.

Behemoth,
    appears as a monster
    He has great hidden strength.

Let us meditate on the diversity of gifts
of living creatures.

Let us think of people with whom we are in contact.
Some may appear to have little to offer. It is
important to look for and recognize
the particular gifts they have.

Some may belong to different cultures or traditions.
It is possible to accept and to learn from them.

Let us think of groups to which we belong. The
particular different gifts each individual person has
to offer can be recognized and used.

Let us think of the Church in its
different manifestations:
local, denominational, universal.
The Church should be ready to recognize
and learn from the different groups
and traditions others have to offer.

The ostrich ... the horses ...
an eagle ... the monster.

Job 39: 14, 24, 27; 40: 15

61

Support from Friends and from Jesus

A man was paralysed. He could not achieve what he wanted. Through the support of four friends he was enabled to hear Jesus saying to him, 'Your sins are forgiven, my friend' and 'Get up and go home.'

Let us think of times in the past
when we have been paralysed,
and unable to do what we wanted.
Let us remember those who in different ways
brought us to Jesus
so that we could hear him saying to us,
'Your sins are forgiven my friend';
and 'Get up and walk'.
Let us give thanks for those friends.

If we feel in any way paralysed,
now or in the future,
let us remember that there are many
both known and unknown
who are bringing us to Jesus in prayer.
Let us also listen again to the words spoken
to the paralysed man.
'Your sins are forgiven my friend';
and 'Get up and walk'.

Let us think of others unable to walk in
the ways of Jesus.
Let us in our prayers carry them to Jesus
so that they too may hear spoken to them
the words of Jesus to the man who could not
walk.

'Your sins are forgiven, my friend';
and 'Get up and walk'.

*Let him down on his bed
into the middle of the group.*

LUKE 5: 19

The Coming of Jesus

The disciples were in a boat making no headway because of the strong wind. They were 'all at sea'. Jesus was on land watching. Seeing their predicament, he came towards them, but they did not recognize him. When he came up to them, they heard him say, 'Courage! It is I. Don't be afraid!'

When we feel that we are getting nowhere, and that we are 'all at sea', let us remember that Jesus is watching from the shore of heaven, and that many are watching with him.

Let us think of individuals or groups who are 'all at sea' and pray that they may know that Jesus is watching them with loving and caring eyes.

Jesus is not only watching, but he is still coming as he did at the first Christmas.

Let us open our eyes to see him as he comes to us. Let us pray that individuals and groups in need may have their eyes opened to see him, as he comes to them.

Let us listen to him speaking 'Courage. It is I. Be not afraid', and discover what these words mean for us today.

Let us pray that individuals and groups who need to hear those words may do so.

Let us look back to those times when we have been making headway, and then have recognized his coming, have heard his voice, and have received his courage.
Let us give thanks for these comings of Jesus.

'It's a ghost!' they thought. Jesus spoke to them at once, 'Courage!' he said. 'It is I. Don't be afraid!'

MARK 6: 49 - 50

Receiving and Giving Strength

The strong are encouraged not to carry the burdens
of the weak
but to give them power to do so.

We are both strong and weak.
In our strength we can give power to others.
In our weakness we can receive power from others.

Let us recall and give thanks that both
in the past and in the present
we have been given strength by others.

Let us think of our contacts that we
may become more aware of any
who may need our help to carry their burdens,
and that we may know how to do so.

Let us think of any individuals or groups
in our own country or in the world who
are carrying burdens,
that we may discover how the strong
can help them to carry those burdens.

Let those of us who are Members,
Associates and Friends of the Community
give thanks for the help we have received
through the prayers of the others,
and for the privilege we have been given
to pray regularly for them.

*We who are strong in the faith ought to
help the weak to carry their burdens.*

ROMANS 15: 1

Growth II

Let us give thanks for those examples we know
where God has given great growth
from small beginnings in church and society.
Let us pray that good life in church and society
which appears to be small
now may have big growth.
'I will cut down the tall trees
and make the small trees grow'.
Let us give thanks for those examples we know
where the small and powerless
have been enabled to grow.
Let us pray for those whom we know
in church and society who are small and powerless
that they may grow.

'Birds of every kind will live there.'

Let us give thanks for all the examples we know
in church and society,
where humans of every kind
have found a welcome and shelter together.

Let us pray that wherever in church and society
humans of diverse kinds do not find a welcome
they may do so.

'I, The Lord have spoken.
I will do what I have said I would do.'

EZEKIEL 17: 24

Let us rejoice and receive strength from this
promise of God.

I will break off a tender sprout;
I will plant it on a high mountain.
It will grow branches and bear seed
and become a magnificent cedar.
Birds of every kind will live there.

EZEKIEL 17: 22, 23

The Shepherd and the Sheep

The little frisky lambs frolic in the sun. They are free enough to enjoy their life and to express their joy. Little children do the same. The older we get the more serious we become, forgetting that Jesus told us to change and become like children.

The sun shines, the rain waters the earth and the green grass grows. The sheep are fed. The bread is broken, the red wine is poured out, and the children are filled with new life.

The sheep hear the calls of the wild animals in the distance and they are afraid. The shepherd knows how to protect them. Wild and dangerous ideas and feelings try to gain entrance into our lives.

The shepherd can protect us from these agents of the devil.

The sheep has wandered away from the flock. It discovers that it is alone, in danger. The shepherd steadily climbs the hillside, systematically searching. At last the sheep is found and brought home to the security of the flock. Many times we have strayed away and have realized that we are lost.

Always the shepherd has come looking for us. Always he has found us.

On the steep rocky hillside the sheep slipped and broke its leg. It could not get up. The shepherd came over to see what was wrong. He bandaged up the leg and the sheep got up and started to walk.

We too have been ill. The shepherd healed us.

Some sheep are weak. When the flock reaches the green grass, they are pushed aside by their stronger neighbours. They cannot get to the best grass. The shepherd is always on the watch. He knows what is happening. He gives them special attention.

The shepherd is watching over us all the time.

I myself will be the shepherd of my sheep, and I will find them a place to rest. I, the sovereign Lord, have spoken. I will look for those that wander off, bandage those that are hurt, and heal those that are sick.

Ezekiel 34: 15, 16

Prayer,

Great shepherd,
When I have been lost
you have always looked for me
and found me and brought me home.
When forces of evil have tried to enter my life
you have protected me.
When I have been ill
you have healed me.
When I have been hungry
you have fed me with the bread of life.
When I have been thirsty
you have offered me life-giving wine.
Keep me in peace
knowing that you are always watching over me.

The Storms of Life

The wind has risen. The waves are high. Water is pouring over the sides of the boat. The boat is being driven along at great speed — nothing can stop it. Rocks loom up ahead. Disaster seems inevitable.

Work is piling up. There is more and more left undone. Will I ever get out of this muddle? I am a failure.

My wife has had a stroke, and she cannot speak. The marriage of my son has broken down. I have had an operation, and the tests have shown that the growth was malignant. One thing after another. What next? What have I done to deserve all this? My God, why have you forsaken me? Where did I read that before? Who spoke it?

Jesus.

I am not alone. He also has been through it. He is in the storm with me. He knows how I feel.

Things will work out, though I do not know how. I can leave the future in his hands.

The calm will come again.

Prayer,

Lord Jesus, the storms of life are overwhelming me. I have kept going until now, but I cannot carry on much longer. You are with me. In your life on earth you had to face even greater storms than I have had to do, and you did not give in but carried on to the end till your work was completely finished. You were able to bring good out of evil. Give me strength to carry on and bring me through the storms to calm. I commit myself and my future into your hands.

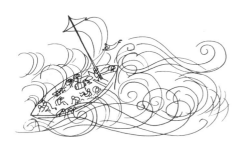

Suddenly a strong wind blew up, and the waves began to spill over into the boat, so that it was about to fill with water. Jesus was in the back of the boat asleep on a pillow. The disciples woke him and said, 'Teacher, don't you care that we are about to die?'
Jesus stood up and commanded the wind, 'Be quiet!' and he said to the waves, 'Be still'. The wind died down, and there was a great calm. Then Jesus said to his disciples, 'Why are you frightened? Have you still no faith?'

MARK 4: 37 - 40

A Safe Refuge

Life is too hot.
I have applied for so many jobs.
Always the same question
'What experience have you got?'
How can I get that experience if
no one will give me a job!
I go home at night just when my pals do;
there is always a row that I am too late.
Why can't my mum understand me,
as other mums do?
Why are there always rows. I hate them.
Does no one understand me?
Take me to a refuge where
I can be understood.

Jesus understands.

The burdens I carry are heavy. The children get on
my nerves. Always they leave their rooms untidy.
There is always somewhere to take them. I am just
a taxi driver. My mother expects to see me every
day. She is always telling me how much she did for
me when I was young. She complains when I have
to leave her.

Take me to a refuge where I can find quiet and time
for prayer and meditation.

Jesus listens.

Work is too hot.
My colleagues misunderstand what I say. They do
not share my vision. I worked hard to get that
contract, harder than the others; but my bonus was
less than theirs. I can't escape. Take me to a refuge
where I can regain the true perspective.

Jesus guides.

Burdens are heavy. I am tired. I don't seem to be
achieving anything. Is it worth carrying on? Take me
to a refuge where I can regain my vision,
my enthusiasm, and my strength.

Jesus refreshes.

Hear my cry, O God;
listen to my prayer!
In despair and far from home
I call to you!

Take me to a safe refuge,
for you are my protector
my strong defence against my enemies.

PSALM 61: 1 - 3

Prayer,

Lord Jesus, we feel lonely and misunderstood. We work hard but our efforts are not appreciated. We have had high hopes in the past, but they have been dashed by failure. Today, we trust in your promise that you will be with us always. Give us, we pray, both today and in all the days ahead, guidance and strength, for without you we can do nothing.

Freedom

Slaves are shackled so that
they cannot move freely.
With freedom comes the possibility
of creative activity.

We can live as slaves to a God who is always waiting
to judge us when we fail. Or we can live as children
of a Father, joyfully sharing in his work.

Our service is then part of freedom.

Throughout the different stages of our life different
pressures can restrain us. In youth uncertainty, due
to inexperience, can deter effective action. In later
life the demands of our work, the demands of our
children, the demands of aged relatives can wear us
out. At all times the frustrations of illness or
disability, and, in old age, the dependence on others
can make us bad tempered.

At all times Jesus is offering to share with us his life.
In accepting that offer we are freed to overcome
these pressures.

The world presses upon us,
to mould us into conformity.
In the world there is the falsity of
racialism, nationalism, and materialism.
In the knowledge that we are all
children of the one God,
we can accept men and women of all races and of
all nations as our brothers and sisters and we are
freed from the falsity of
nationalism and racialism.

In the knowledge of everlasting life,
and of what belongs to that life,
we are freed from the falsity of materialism.

The fear of death can enslave us.
But at Easter Jesus lived again.
In that knowledge we are freed
to live the new and eternal life
which death cannot destroy.

We are freed from the fear of death.

*So then, you are no longer a slave but a son or
daughter. And since that is what you are, God
will give you all that he has for his heirs.*

GALATIANS 4: 7

71

Prayer,

Jesus Christ, we open our lives to you.
So fill us, we pray, with your Spirit that there is no
room left for the spirit of the world.
Give us life and courage
that we may be able to overcome
all the trials that come to defeat us.
Free us from all that hinders us that
we may serve you to the end.

Serving Others

Four figures. Two irrelevant in the background.
Two important in the foreground.

The Priest and Levite on their way
to the temple:
afraid that bandits may still be near;
apprehensive of possible defilement by touching
the victim who may be dead.

The Victim:
depressed
humiliated
in danger of death.

The Stranger:
a Samaritan nevertheless a neighbour to a Jew.

How frequently can we identify with these figures?

The Priest and Levite: afraid of taking risks.
Concerned with religious duties,
yet missing human need.

The Victim:
depressed
rejected
in danger of death.

The Stranger:
Loving and serving.

Which figures represent Jesus?

The Victim:
with arms outstretched as on a cross.

The Stranger:
with arms enfolding in love and healing.

Prayer,

Jesus forgive us when we pass the victim by.
Jesus help us to see you in all victims,
and enable us to love and serve them.
Jesus, when we are depressed
unloved
in danger of death,
help us to feel your arms around us.

The Good Samaritan

His heart was filled with pity.

Luke 10: 33

75

Supporting the Weak

Many are weak some of the time; some are weak all of the time.
Some are physically weak through illness,
or through disability.

Some are mentally weak. Many have not reached their potential because they have not been enabled to do so.

Some are psychologically weak, on account of the experiences through which they have passed. Insecurity in their childhood may have led to imagined hostility on the part of others —
an insecurity which has led to assertiveness.

Some have spiritual weakness — perhaps caused by what appears to be undeserved suffering —
perhaps because of apparent rejection by an uncaring person or group.

There is much weakness in the world.
Weakness which is admitted —
weakness which is hidden —
weakness which is disguised —
weakness which is denied.

Those who are strong can share with those who are weak, so that the weak become strong.

Prayer,

Help us, O God, to understand others,
to see behind the outward words and actions the person that they really are,
to accept them
and then to assist them to become the person you have planned them to be.

We who are strong in the faith ought to help the weak to carry their burdens.

Romans 15: 1

Sharing Burdens

Some have the burden of being outsiders,
of belonging to some despised group.
If they are treated with dignity,
then their burden is lightened.

Some have disabilities in body, mind or spirit.
Important help can be given
through prayer for healing.
But healing does not always
come in the way desired.
Encouragement can be offered.
Patience can be shown.

Some carry the burden of sin and guilt.
God offers forgiveness but forgiveness
must be wanted and accepted.
Can a person experience
the forgiveness of God
if they have not experienced human forgiveness?
'If you forgive people's sins, they are forgiven;
if you do not forgive them, they are not forgiven.'
We can help to lift the burden of guilt by
accepting them, by forgiving them, by encouraging
them to accept forgiveness.

Some burdens can be carried
only by corporate action.
Is there sufficient corporate sharing of burdens
in our local Christian group?

Is the state sharing burdens as fully as it might?

Are we ourselves carrying heavy burdens?
Are we allowing others
to help us to carry them?
Are we holding on to burdens of office,
which we should allow others to carry now?

Prayer,

Lord Jesus, you needed Simon to carry your cross.
Help us to see who and how we can help to carry
the burdens which others have to bear. When
burdened ourselves, give us the humility to accept
the help which others offer to us.

*Help to carry one another's burdens, and in
this way you will obey the law of Christ.*

GALATIANS 6: 2

77

Service

When the lame man saw Peter and John going into the temple, he begged them to give him something. They looked straight at him, and Peter said, 'Look at us!' So he looked at them expecting to get something from them. But Peter said to him, 'I have no money at all, but I give you what I have: in the name of the Lord Jesus Christ of Nazareth I order you to get up and walk!' Then he took him by his right hand and helped him up. At once the man's feet and ankles became strong; he jumped up, stood on his feet, and started walking around.

Acts 3: 3 - 8

The lame beggar was unknown to Peter and John. They could easily have walked past him. They stopped and spoke to him, and answered his cry for help not in the way that he had expected, but in the only way that they could.

It is all too easy to be blind to the needs of others, and in particular to the needs of strangers. Some old people die while those who might have been able to help have been unaware of their needs. Other people take their own lives, when those around them have been unaware of the turmoil going on within them.

We need to pray for sensitivity towards the needs of others.

Peter did not offer the man money. He had none to give. He offered him the faith that through the power of Jesus he could walk. 'In the name of the Lord Jesus Christ of Nazareth, I order you to get up and walk.' And he did.

It is very easy to see weaknesses in others. It is easy to criticize them. What is really needed is to help them to draw on the power of Jesus to overcome their weaknesses.

'I give you what I have.'

The needs of the other may be for money, food or goods of one kind or another. That may be the appropriate gift and we may be able to give it.

Christians in other lands,
in changing circumstances,
continue to look to us for interest
and shared concern.
Whatever else we have to offer,
we can always offer our prayers,
which are as important as any other gift.

Prayer,

Lord Jesus, help us to be sensitive to the needs of those around us.
Make us willing to offer them what we have and they need.

Hospitality

The publicity of the Church is based on 'welcome'. There is nothing new about this. Welcome has always been a mark of the Church.

We think of visits we have paid to other congregations: what kind of welcome did we receive! We think of our own congregation: what kind of welcome do others receive when they come?

Does our welcome extend to all kinds of people? Does it include people of all races and from all countries?

The telephone rings when we are busy. The caller may have some urgent need to speak to us. It is not always easy to give a friendly answer, and a listening ear.

The door bell rings. The unexpected stranger stands on the doorstep. At this moment he is not welcome, but he must not know it.

Old communities are extended families. There is not much that is not known, and everyone has his or her place and belongs. How different is the new community! Strangers live beside one another and remain strangers. We can be amongst those who change strangers into neighbours.

To our country there come visitors to stay differing lengths of time. In the past many have come and have stayed and have felt at home. In recent years many have come and have not felt at home and have become alienated.

Hospitality should still be a mark of the Church. 'Receive him then, with joy, as a brother in the Lord.'

Prayer,

Heavenly Father, in the past we have been enriched by those whom we have welcomed,
and to whom we have offered hospitality.
It has not always been easy and it is not easy now.
Help us we pray, to welcome strangers, and to transform them into neighbours,
that they may feel at home.

*Receive him then, with joy,
as a brother in the Lord.*

PHILIPPIANS 2: 29

79

Bread

They found him in the Temple, sitting with the Jewish teachers, listening to them and asking questions.

Luke 2: 46

They all ate and had enough.

Luke 9: 17

Jesus told them, 'I am the Bread of Life.'

John 6: 35

Many in the world are hungry for bread — some are so hungry that they die. Many are hungry for work — some are so hungry that their marriages break down.

Many are hungry for recognition — some are so hungry that they rebel to attract attention.
How can the hungry be fed?
Can we share more?
Can we help to change the policies of societies and nations?

Many are hungry for the bread of life.
Some do not know the reason for their hunger.
Some do not know how their hunger can be satisfied.

There is a free offer of the bread of life.
This offer can be rejected or it can be accepted.
We can be the means of sharing the bread of life.

Prayer,

Heavenly Father, we thank you for the world and for all that grows in it. Prevent us from wasting its produce, and help us to discover how it might produce more.
Teach us that the fruits of the earth belong to you and are your gifts to us,
to use for the life of all your children.
Make us hungry for the Word of life,
and, being fed, help us to share that life with others.

Old Age

I never thought that it would happen to me.

I am ashamed — lifelong friends and I cannot remember their names!
What will they think of me!

I used to help others. Now I need their help! I can't even get out of my chair without help. Walking down the street everyone passes me. I took pride in doing a good day's work. Now I just sit back tired, when there is so much to do.

What has God left for me?

Dependence!
That is just the problem. I used to be so independent. I took pride in doing things for myself. Now I must depend on others. I don't like it. Perhaps dependence is a gift I am too proud to take. My dependence gives to others the opportunity to serve.
I have always found it harder to receive service than to give it. I must learn to receive with thanks, and so be an example to others.

Has God given me anything else?

Time.
Indeed, too much time. I used to be so busy I never had enough time.
Now I have so much time. How can I use it?
More time for prayer. I never used to find enough time for prayer, there was so much to do. So many in the world today are like I used to be.
They are very busy; they do not find it easy to pray. I can pray for them. I can pray for all the many people who need my prayers.

Is that all that God has given me?

The most important thing — I still have the knowledge of his presence with me. This knowledge I can share with others, and especially with the young. They are more ready to learn from one of my age than from those who are younger than I am.

You have taught me ever since I was young,
and I still tell of your wonderful acts.
Now that I am old and my hair is grey,
do not abandon me, O God!
Be with me while I proclaim your power
and might to all generations to come.

PSALM 71: 17 - 18

81

Prayer,

Ever-present Father, You are still as near to me now as you have been in the past. Help me to know that you still have much for me to do.

Help me to pray for others, and especially for those who do not pray for themselves. Teach me humility, to accept thankfully service from others, and by that joyful dependence to teach others to be dependent on you.
Help me to pass on to young people the good news you have shared with me.

So may I go on serving you to the end.

The Church

Difficult Choices

As children Simon and Andrew had often watched their father fishing. As they grew older they had helped him. They well remembered the day when he had first trusted them to go out on their own. They were still fishermen. Fishing was their livelihood. Fishing was their life.

They had listened to Jesus speaking. They did so as often as they could. They had been excited by his words. They had been even more excited by his presence. Now he was asking them to help him in his work.

What a choice!

Continuing with what they had always done. Continuing with what they enjoyed doing or leaving fishing and going with Jesus.

The choice was not easy. Fishing was healthy. Fishing provided food for men and women to eat. There was nothing wrong with fishing. Continue fishing and listen to Jesus as often as they could. That would have been a good compromise.

But it was not what Jesus wanted.

It is easy to choose between two ways when one is clearly right and the other clearly wrong. It is not easy when both alternatives are good. It is always possible to find good reasons for doing what is wrong. Andrew and Simon might have done that. But they left their nets.

What are the things to which people cling? What are the things which people find hard to leave behind? Home and family. Children. Possessions. Privacy. Job.

Prayer,

Jesus, our leader, there are many things you have asked us to leave behind. We thank you for giving us the strength to do so. In days ahead, guide us in all choices that we must make. Release us from so closely clinging to past ways, that we are not free to follow you into the future.

As Jesus walked along the shore of Lake Galilee, he saw two fishermen, Simon and his brother Andrew, catching fish with a net. Jesus said to them, 'Come with me, and I will teach you to catch people'. At once they left their nets and went with him.

MARK 1: 16 - 18

Resurrection Life of the Church

What is true of the Church immediately after the resurrection is still true of the Church today.

The net can picture the Church, and the fish in it the members of the Church. Disciples are not only followers of Jesus but also fishers of men and women.

During the night, the disciples caught no fish. The net was empty. In the morning they caught many and the net was full. During the night they fished under their own plan. In the morning they fished according to the instructions of Jesus.

Let us think whether we and the Church are fishing according to the instructions of Jesus.

Jesus stood on the shore.
At first they did not recognize him.
Then John said 'It is the Lord'.
Jesus can be present in the words of others.
Jesus can be at work in their actions.
Are we recognizing what he is saying and doing?

Jesus has prepared a meal for them,
and invited them to share it with him.
At communion do we recognize in what the celebrant says and does the presence of Jesus speaking to us and acting for us?

The net contains many different kinds of fish and never breaks. It is one net.
Is this true of the Church today?
If not, how can we help to enable it to become true?

Simon Peter dragged the net ashore.

JOHN 21: 11

The temple is destroyed.
Many of God's people are away in exile in Babylon.
Ezekiel had a vision of a new day.
He is shown round the new temple.
He sees the light of God shining into it.
He sees the water of life flowing from it
into the world.
The name of the city from now on is
'The Lord is here'.

The Church is struggling.
Nearly all statistics of the Church in Britain
have a downward trend.
Many of its members are in exile.

Let us be encouraged by the vision of Ezekiel.
He saw a new temple.
Let us reflect on what are the present needs
in the life of the Church,
and upon what the plan and structure
of a renewed Church will be.

'The light of God will shine on it.'
Let us meditate on how we alone
or in company with others can see the light;
and how the exiles may be enabled to see it.

The water of life will flow from the
Church into the world.
Let us meditate on how we will enable the water
of life to flow from the Church into the world'.

Let us rejoice that the name of the city
and of the Church will be:

'The Lord is here'.

EZEKIEL 48: 35

Vision of a New Day for the Church

*He was holding a linen tape measure
and measuring rod.*

EZEKIEL 40: 3

*The dazzling light passed
through the east gate.*

EZEKIEL 43: 4

*The man told me to wade
through the stream there.*

EZEKIEL 47: 3

The Valley of Dry Bones

He said to me, 'Mortal man,
can these bones come back to life?'
I replied, 'Sovereign Lord,
only you can answer that.'
He said, 'Tell these dry bones to listen
to the word of the Lord.
Tell them that I, the Sovereign Lord,
am saying to them:
"I am going to put breath into you
and bring you back to life".'

Let us think of those times
that we felt depressed and lifeless.
The Spirit of God breathed on us
and gave us new life.
Let us give thanks to God.
If at present we feel lifeless,
let us in confidence be open to
the coming of the Spirit of God.

Let us meditate on the Church.
It is both full of life and also of dry bones.
Where it is dry let us pray that the wind of God
may blow on it to give it new life.

Let us pray for all who will be visiting Iona this
year that the wind of God may blow on them.

There are many valleys of dry bones in the world:
areas of war and conflict
areas of oppression
areas of deprivation
areas of great shortages of food or water
areas of isolation such as prisons.

Let us pray that the Spirit of God
may blow on them to bring them new life.

I could see that there were very many bones.

Ezekiel 37: 2

The Peacemakers

The devil is the great divider;
God is the great uniter;
therefore are the peacemakers
called the children of God.
There is great variety in humanity.
Variety in culture
— variety in appearance
— variety of food
— variety of personality
— variety of music ...

It is possible to rejoice
in others who are different from us.
It is possible to rejoice
in the spirituality of others,
which may be very different from our own.
The aged can rejoice
in the enthusiasms of the young;
The young can rejoice
in the quiet peace of the aged.

Differences and divisions do exist
and must be faced.
Confrontation increases conflict;
search for mutual understanding
leads to peace.
Blessed are the peacemakers.

Prayer,

Lord, make us instruments of thy peace.
Where there is hatred, let us sow love
where there is injury, pardon
where there is discord, union
where there is doubt, faith
where there is despair, hope
where there is darkness, light
where there is sadness, joy
for thy mercy and for thy truth's sake.

PRAYER ATTRIBUTED TO ST FRANCIS OF ASSISI

*How wonderful it is, how pleasant, for God's
people to live together in harmony!*

PSALM 133: 1

*This plan, which God will complete when the
time is right, is to bring all creation together,
everything in heaven and on earth,
with Christ as head.*

EPHESIANS 1: 10

89

Togetherness Round the Table

Jesus is present with us
round the table as host.
We share with each other because
he has first shared with us.

Let us think of all in our own church,
including those with whom we differ,
and realize that Jesus unites us with them.
Let us pray that we may be open to them
and that they may be open to us.

Jesus is present as host at the tables
of all the different churches.
Let us realize that Jesus
is sharing the same loaf with them
as he does with us,
and pray that we may be open to them
and that they may be open to us.

Jesus is present as host at tables in all the
different parts of the world,
sharing the same loaf with them
as he does with us.
Let us pray that we may discover
how to share spiritual insights
and also bodily needs.

Jesus is present at the table in heaven
united with those who have ended
their life on earth,
including those whom we loved
and who loved us when they lived here.
Let us realize that round the table
we continue to share the loaf with them.

We all share the same loaf.

1 CORINTHIANS 10: 17

90

Growth III

The plant grows. It had to be planted.
It had to be watered.
Planting and watering are different
but both are needed.
But it is God who makes the plant grow.

Let us think of the Iona Community.
George MacLeod planted it. Many Members,
Associates, Friends and others have watered it.
But it is God who has made it grow.

Let us pray that it may continue to be watered
and that God may continue to make it grow.

Let us think about the whole Church.
Jesus planted it.
Many through the ages have watered it.
It has been God who has made it grow.
Let us pray that it may continue to be watered,
and that God will make it grow.
Let us think of those groups
who have shared common interests
or who have engaged on common tasks.
Individuals or groups have founded them,
and many have watered them.
God has given the growth.
Let us pray for continuing watering in the future
and that God will give them growth.

God made the plant grow.

1 Corinthians 3: 6

91

Bearing the Cross II

Let us meditate on this picture.

Is it a picture of the Church? If so, how much does the Church today resemble it?

Jesus is out in front, and the others follow in his steps. Jesus is ahead leading into new ways.
Is the Church following him?

In this picture Jesus is also in the midst of the others carrying his cross. He enables them to carry their crosses as he gives to them the broken bread.

Let us meditate on the cross we carry. We are supported not only by Jesus, but also by the others who are around us carrying their crosses.

Who are carrying crosses? Not only those who are members of the Church, but also many others who do not realize that they are following Jesus.

He must forget self, carry his cross,
and follow me.

MARK 8: 34

Unity of the Family of God

The seeds of wheat are ground together. Each portion of bread comes from many seeds. The one loaf of bread is given to many different people. The portion which each receives is part of the one loaf. Unity and diversity are bound together.

Do we feel that we belong together? Do we feel that we belong to all Christian communities in our own town or district, or do we just belong to one?

We recognize that worship with others in our own church is part of our life. We know we need to meet not only with Jesus, but also with those who are his brothers and sisters. Do we also know that the same need extends to meeting with his brothers and sisters who are not members of our own particular Christian group?

Unity has been maintained by Christians divided by war. Unity has been maintained by Christians of different races and of different colours. Unity has been maintained between Christians whose understanding of the Christian faith has differed.

This unity has to be expressed and must be seen to exist. Greet one another with the kiss of Christian love.

We should never do apart things which we can do together.

Tragically, joint Christian worship and action have not always been given the importance that they deserve. It has too often been left to the few. Worship and action with Christians of different traditions are something that all followers of Jesus should take seriously.

Because there is one loaf of bread, all of us, though many, are one body, for we all share the same loaf.

1 CORINTHIANS 10: 17

So there is no difference between Jews and Gentiles, between slaves and free people, between men and women; you are all one in Christ Jesus.

GALATIANS 3: 28

Greet one another with the kiss of Christian love.

1 PETER 5: 14

93

Prayer,

Jesus shares one loaf with us.
We are one in Christ.
We express our unity in Christian love.

Lord Jesus we rejoice that in our baptism
you united yourself with us and that you thereby
united us with all your brothers and sisters.
We rejoice that through baptism
you have bridged all earthly divisions.
Help us to see how we can express our unity,
and give us power to embody that vision.

When Jacob went to sleep he was not aware of the presence of God. The unexpected happened. 'The Lord is in this place.'

Let us recall with thanks the places and times when we have had similar experiences.

At times when we share the experience of Jacob, that we do not know the presence of God, we can recall in imagination the times and places when we have known that God was present, so that the miracle can happen again.

Can we think of those known or unknown who have not known the nearness of God, and pray that the same miracle that happened for Jacob may happen for them?

Angels came down bringing messages from God. Who accompanies them?

Those whom we have known and loved on earth; those who have challenged and supported us.

Angels go up to heaven
taking our prayers with them.

Who goes with them?

Do we, even while we live on earth?

The table of the Lord is the same table on earth as in heaven. When we share round the table we join not only those round the table on earth, but also those round the table in heaven.

There is two-way traffic on the ladder.
From heaven to earth and from earth to heaven.

Jesus came down the ladder to the very depths to find all there and to take them up to the height.

Endpiece
A Stairway from
Earth to Heaven

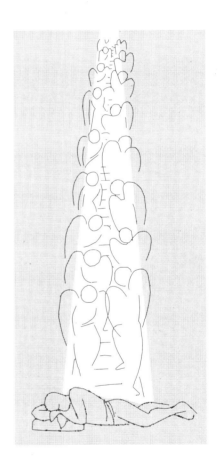

Jacob woke up and said, 'The Lord is here! He is in this place, and I didn't know it.' He was afraid and said, 'What a terrifying place this is! It must be the house of God; it must be the gate that opens into heaven.'

GENESIS 28: 16, 17

95